MEGAFAST
TRUCKS

Thanks to the creative team:
Senior Editor: Alice Peebles
Designer: Lauren Woods and collaborate agency

Original edition copyright 2015 by Hungry
Tomato Ltd.

Hungry Tomato™
A division of Lerner Publishing Group, Inc.
241 First Avenue North
Minneapolis, MN 55401 USA

For reading levels and more information, look up
this title at www.lernerbooks.com.

Main body text set in Economica Bold.
Typeface provided by Tipotype.

**Library of Congress Cataloging-in-Publication
Data**

The Cataloging-in-Publication Data for *Megafast
Trucks* is on file at the Library of Congress.

ISBN 978-1-4677-9366-7 (lib. bdg.)
ISBN 978-1-4677-9587-6 (pbk.)
ISBN 978-1-4677-9588-3 (EB pdf)

Manufactured in the United States of America
1 – VP – 12/31/15

MEGAFAST TRUCKS

by John Farndon
Illustrated by Mat Edwards and Jeremy Pyke

HUNGRY
TOMATO™

CONTENTS

MEGAFAST TRUCKS

Trucks aren't meant to be fast, are they? Just big and strong, or simply hardworking. Wrong. As this book shows, some trucks are megafast. And when big trucks go fast, hurling their massive bulk along road or track, the sight is truly spectacular. Imagine a giant truck roaring along faster than a Formula One racing car, or jumping huge distances through the air. In this book, we'll introduce some trucks that do just that.

TRUCKIN' JOCHEN

Some say the greatest truck racing driver of all time is the German Jochen Hahn. Jochen's dad, Konrad Hahn, was a champion truck racing driver too, and creator of the Hahn racing team. In 1999, Konrad had a bad crash, and Jochen became the team's lead driver. Jochen's results got better and better, and in 2011, 2012, and 2013 he and the team were European Truck Racing champions three times in a row.

ROAD SPEEDS

Once, track racing was just for lightweight cars and bikes. But in the last few decades all kinds of trucks have joined in the fun—giant Arctic rigs, pickups, monster-tired stunt wagons, off-roaders, fire engines, school buses… You name a kind of truck, and almost certainly someone, somewhere, will be racing it.

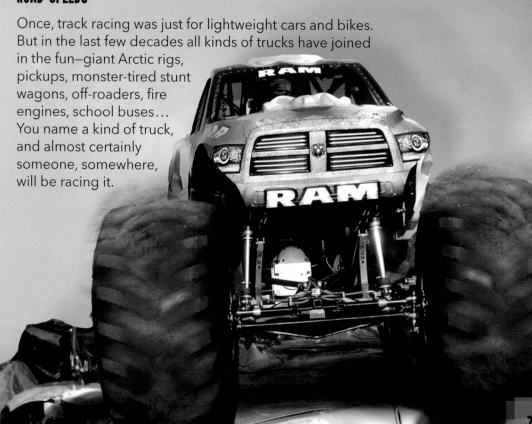

THAT WAS HOW FAST?!

It is easy to see when a plane or a motorcycle, a car or a truck is megafast. But *how* do you know just how fast it is? Speed is the distance that something moves in a certain time. It is the distance covered divided by the time. If a jet plane travels 2,000 miles in two hours, it travels 1,000 miles in each hour. So we say its speed is 1,000 miles per hour, or mph. The top speeds for the machines in this book are given in mph.

SPEED MATTERS

Speeds for vehicles on the ground are typically given in mph (miles per hour) or km/h (kilometers per hour). Rockets may soar away from Earth at over 11 km per second. If a plane flies faster than sound (typically over 700 mph), its speed may be compared to the speed of sound in similar conditions. This speed is called a Mach number. So a plane flying at the speed of sound is said to be flying at Mach 1, at 20 times the speed of sound it's Mach 20, and so on.

GETTING QUICKER

One way of seeing how fast something moves is to measure how quickly it gains speed—that is, its acceleration. You can actually measure how much something accelerates every second. But with fast vehicles, the acceleration is usually given by how long it takes to reach a particular speed, typically from a standing start, 0 mph. The shorter the time, the faster the acceleration. So acceleration figures for a superbike that takes just 2.9 seconds to get from a standstill to 60 mph would be 0-60 in 2.9 seconds. That's megafast!

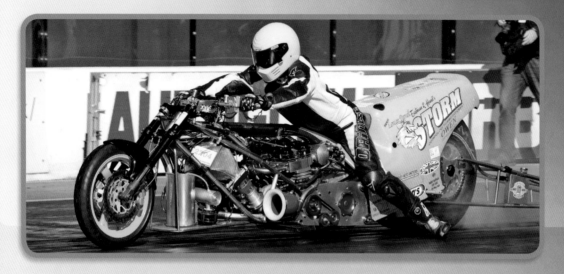

AGAINST THE CLOCK

The most accurate way of measuring top speed is to measure how long a vehicle takes to cover an exact distance, such as a mile. That's how the official top speeds in this book were measured. To ensure split-second accuracy, the clock is triggered to start and stop when the vehicle cuts through a beam of light.

SPEED DIAL

Speed against the clock is average speed. Police speed guns and speedometers in cars, trucks, and motorcycles register the speed at any one instant. Speed guns fire a radar beam and detect the way it bounces off the moving vehicle. With speedometers, an electronic sensor counts the number of times small magnets on the wheel sweep past it each second and converts this into a speed in mph to display on a vehicle's dashboard or LCD screen.

FASTER THAN A JET PLANE

Les Shockley's Shockwave has to be the most amazing truck ever. From the front it looks like an ordinary 1984 Peterbilt truck. But mounted on the back are three Pratt & Whitney jet engines that blast this fire-breathing monster from a standstill to 300 mph in just 11 seconds. And it can actually scorch along at 376 mph!

CATCH THAT JET!

In demonstrations at air shows, a jet fighter flies low over a standing Shockwave. Instantly Shockwave roars into life. Within just a quarter of a mile it has not only caught up with the plane but actually overtaken it! The truck does have brakes, but it throws out parachutes to help it slow down again. On each run, Shockwave burns through about 400 gallons of jet fuel.

Top Speed	50	100	200

FLAMING FURY

Father-and-son team Neal and Chris Darnell rebuilt Shockwave in 2012 and know how to put on a show. The flames that gush from the twin exhaust stacks on the cab are not really part of the jet. They are fed with raw diesel fuel, then electrically ignited to produce spectacular flame effects as Shockwave gets ready.

POWER
36,000 bhp

0–300 MPH
11 seconds

TOP SPEED
376 mph

ENGINE
Three Pratt & Whitney J34-48 jet engines

THRUST
19,000 lb

PRICE
Unknown

300	400	500	376 mph

ROARING RAM AND MONSTER MUNCH

Who said wheels have to be small? "Bigfoot" monster trucks have giant wheels, massive suspensions, and super-powerful engines that enable them to charge over obstacles and perform breathtaking stunts. They can drive over cars, bounce over ditches, and actually leap through the air. No wonder millions of people turn up for Monster Jam events.

FLYING TRUCK!

Monster trucks compete ferociously for the longest jump. But Joe Sylvester's truck Bad Habit soars the farthest of all. In 2013, Bad Habit charged up the launch ramp at 85 mph and then hurtled 237.5 ft through the air before landing almost on its nose. That amazing leap demolished the previous world record of 214.67 ft.

Top Speed

| 50 | 100 | 200 |

RAMINATOR

When brothers Tim and Mark Hall set out to build the Raminator, they didn't just want a stunt master—they wanted a truck with superpower. What they came up with is the world's fastest bigfoot. Raminator reached a sensational world record of 99.1 mph in December 2014, ripping up the Circuit of the Americas in Austin, Texas.

POWER
Over 2,000 bhp

0-60 MPH
3 seconds

TOP SPEED
99.1 mph

ENGINE
3-port M26MB nitro engine

TORQUE
865 lb-ft max

PRICE
Unknown

300   400   500   **99.1 mph**

PICKUP RACER

You may think a pickup is just for hauling around a load of supplies. Hot rodder Gale Banks will make you think again. His Sidewinder Dodge Dakota pickup not only looks as sleek and shiny as any supercar, it's superfast, too, and in 2002 it set a world record for pickups at 217 mph.

Top Speed

| 50 | 100 | 200 |

DON'T STEP ON THIS SNAKE!

Sidewinders are venomous snakes that live in the deserts of the southwestern USA. These deadly predators have their own special way of moving over the loose desert sand. Instead of moving forwards, they whip sideways so fast they can be hard to see. It seems an apt name for the Banks pickup, which whips across the Bonneville Salt Flats in Utah at high speeds.

POWER
735 bhp

QUARTER MILE
+179 mph

TOP SPEED
217 mph

ENGINE
5.9 liter turbo diesel

TORQUE
1,300 lb-ft

PRICE
$1,000,000

DIESEL DESTROYER

The Banks Sidewinder uses a diesel engine, not a gasoline engine. Banks Engineering were determined to show that diesels could be just as fast as gas engines. They squeezed 735 bhp (brake horsepower) out of a Cummins diesel engine with a special "variable geometry" turbocharger.

300   400   500

217 mph

ROAD RUNNER

The world's fastest-accelerating street-legal car is not a Lamborghini or Bugatti supercar, but a pickup truck. It's Larry Larson's 1998 Chevy S-10, which in 2014 covered a quarter-mile from a standing start in under 6 seconds, reaching over 244 mph. You won't see this superfast truck much on the highway, though. It's a drag racer, built for displaying its might on the strip.

Top Speed

50   100   200

TRUCK TREATMENT

Larson's S-10 gets its power from a Brodix Chevy engine so mighty that the hood needs a bulge to fit it in. The S-10 has two fuel systems: gasoline for the road and pure alcohol for the drag track. When the pickup is on the drag track, the gas system is removed to save weight. The truck's heavy steel doors are also temporarily replaced by light carbon-fiber doors.

POWER
3,500 bhp

0-244.43 MPH
5.95 seconds

TOP SPEED
At least
244.43 mph

ENGINE
10,000cc twin
turbo

TORQUE
580 lb-ft

PRICE
$137,000
(estimated)

FAT AND SLICK

Dragsters look very different from road vehicles because of their massive rear tires. These have no tread, so they are sometimes called "slicks," and they provide the biggest tire area touching the track. This gives good grip or "traction" on a dry track, and allows the engine's power to be used to maximum effect to push the dragster forward.

| 300 | 400 | 500 | 244.43 mph |

RAM SPEED

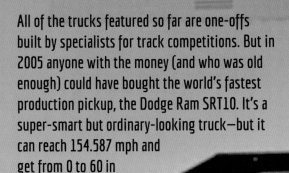

All of the trucks featured so far are one-offs built by specialists for track competitions. But in 2005 anyone with the money (and who was old enough) could have bought the world's fastest production pickup, the Dodge Ram SRT10. It's a super-smart but ordinary-looking truck—but it can reach 154.587 mph and get from 0 to 60 in about 5 seconds!

SUPERLIGHT BODY

When Dodge Ram designed the SRT10, they weren't really looking to pick up pigs on the farm. They used wind-tunnel testing to give it a super-streamlined shape. And they powered it with a muscular 8-liter Chrysler V10 engine. The massive power bulge in the hood is the giveaway of the mighty engine beneath.

Top Speed	50	100	200

DODGY

Dodge cars are simply the division of car manufacturer Chrysler that makes muscle cars. The company was founded back in 1900 by the Dodge brothers, Horace and John. It has nothing to do with Dodge City, which was known at the time for its Wild West toughness. But the Dodge brothers had a Wild West way of doing business—and Dodge cars carry that pioneering frontier spirit with them.

POWER
3,500 bhp

0-60 MPH
4.9 seconds

TOP SPEED
At least
154.587 mph

ENGINE
8300cc V10

TORQUE
525 lb-ft

PRICE
$57,000

300	400	500	**154.5587mph**

FAST AND WILD

Off-roaders are meant to be rugged and ready for any kind of terrain. They're not meant to be fast, right? Well, think again. Ford's F-150 SVT Raptor is a pickup that's both tough in the mud and megafast on roads. Powered by a big V8 engine, it can scream up to 60 mph in just over 6 seconds—almost as fast as a Chevrolet Camaro! Yet it can also cope with anything from desert sand to fresh snow.

Top Speed   50   100   200

RAPTOR

The Raptor gets its name from a family of birds called raptors: birds of prey that include hawks, eagles, falcons, and vultures. These superb fliers have super-sharp eyes for spotting prey from high up. They grasp their prey with their curved talons and rip off flesh with their hooked beaks.

POWER
411 bhp

0-60 MPH
6.5 seconds

TOP SPEED
150 mph

ENGINE
6.5 liter V8

TORQUE
434 lb-ft

PRICE
About
$50,000

TOUGH IN THE DIRT

There are plenty of fast vehicles on the world's roads, but very few speed kings could handle extreme off-road conditions as well as the Raptor. Key to its off-road abilities are a rugged build, four-wheel drive, and extremely long suspension travel. The driver even has Hill Descent Control. This adjusts braking and acceleration automatically to keep the Raptor's speed steady when coming down steep banks.

300   400   500   **150mph**

WHERE'S THE FIRE?

You want fire engines to get to fires fast—but none of them will match Shannen Seydel's Hawaiian Fire Department Eagle. In 1995, Florida firefighter Seydel took the water tank out of a 1940s Ford fire truck and slotted in two Rolls-Royce jet engines in its place to create the world's fastest fire truck. Seydel has never been to Hawaii, nor has his record-breaking truck. He just liked the idea of the place.

| Top Speed | 50 | 100 | 200 |

FASTEST TRUCK EVER

In July 1998, on a track in Ontario, Canada, Seydel unleashed his fire-breathing beast. The speed that his Hawaiian Eagle reached was just astonishing. It burned up to 200 mph in barely 7 seconds and eventually reached a scorching 407 mph. That beat even Shockwave (see pp. 10-11) and stands as a world truck speed record even now.

JET PROPULSION

All jet engines work by drawing air in with a huge fan. As the fan sucks in the air, it squeezes it and mixes it with fuel. The mix is set alight and swells rapidly, shooting out of the back of the engine. The hot air that shoots out hits the air outside and creates thrust—a mighty push that drives the plane (or fire engine!) forward.

POWER
12,000 bhp

0-200 MPH
7 seconds

TOP SPEED
407 mph

ENGINE
Two Rolls-Royce Bristol Viper engines

THRUST
2 x 12,000 lb

PRICE
$57,000

MARK SMITH

UNITED STATES
FIRE DEPT.

| 300 | 400 | 500 | 407mph |

TRUCK RACERS

When truck racing began in the 1980s, the racers were just the cabs of big road-going trucks. Unhooked from their trailers, the cabs could bowl along at speeds of up to 150 mph. People found the sight of these monsters tearing around a track so exciting that the sport caught on. Nowadays, the trucks are purpose-built racers that will never haul load.

Top Speed

| | 50 | 100 | 200 |

RACING RULES

Racing trucks are built to very specific technical requirements to ensure fair competition. They also have to weigh over 6 tons and be limited to 100 mph to keep the sport safe. With monster trucks hurtling along so close together, crashes do happen, but they are usually fairly minor, and injuries to drivers are very rare.

POWER
1,479 bhp

0-60 MPH
Unknown

TOP SPEED
100 mph

ENGINE
8-cylinder
16,500cc

TORQUE
Over 4,056
lb-ft

PRICE
Unknown

THE KISS OF SUCCESS

Trucks are raced by teams, and among the best are KM Racing and Frankie OXXO, both based in the Czech Republic. OXXO's most successful driver, Hungarian Norbert Kiss, won the European Drivers' Championship in 2014 in a German MAN truck.

| 300 | 400 | 500 | **100mph** |

PICKING UP SPEED

It's only been going 20 years or so, but pickup truck racing is already hugely popular. Specially built versions of production pickups race around oval tracks at high speeds in long races. In a typical race in the NASCAR Camping World series, the trucks cover 250 miles in just two hours or so, at average speeds of 110 to 140 mph.

Top Speed | 50 | 100 | 200

NASCAR TRUCKS

Race trucks have the same basic shape as road pickups, but they look very different. To keep on the track when cornering at high speeds, they are built very low, with racing wheels in deeply recessed wheel arches. A deep spoiler at the front and a wing at the back force air down, helping the truck grip the track. Crashes do happen, though…

POWER
500 bhp

0-60 MPH
6 seconds or better

TOP SPEED
140 mph or better

ENGINE
5,700cc V8

TORQUE
550 lb-ft

PRICE
$75,000

FUEL ECONOMY

With such long races, trucks burn a lot of fuel. Though they have big tanks, the winning driver is not necessarily the fastest but often the one who uses fuel best. That was how Matt Crafton won the Toyota Tundra 250 in 2014, creeping over the finish line with his last drop of fuel, while others stopped to refuel.

| 300 | 400 | 500 | **140mph** |

SCHOOL'S OUT!

If you're ever late for school, what you need is School Time from the Indy Boys. School Time looks pretty much like any other school bus. But Indy Boys motorhead and designer Paul Stender stripped out all the seats and replaced them with a 42,000-hp Phantom F-4 fighter-jet engine that can blast the old bus up to 367 mph in a matter of seconds!

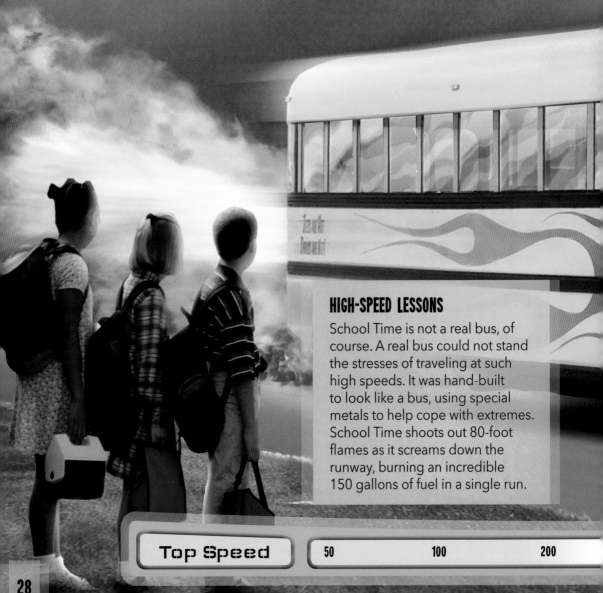

HIGH-SPEED LESSONS

School Time is not a real bus, of course. A real bus could not stand the stresses of traveling at such high speeds. It was hand-built to look like a bus, using special metals to help cope with extremes. School Time shoots out 80-foot flames as it screams down the runway, burning an incredible 150 gallons of fuel in a single run.

Top Speed

| 50 | 100 | 200 |

GHOST SPEED

The McDonnell Phantom F-4 was one of the fastest and most successful jet fighters of the last century, operating from 1960 to 1996. It was famous for the powerful jet engines that helped it to climb at breathtaking speeds. In 1961, a Phantom hurtled through the sky at 1,606.342 mph—a record not beaten for over 15 years.

POWER
42,000 bhp

0-100 MPH
4 seconds or better

TOP SPEED
367 mph

ENGINE
Phantom F-4 jet engine

THRUST
17,900 lb

PRICE
Unknown

300   400   500   **367mph**

WANT TO KNOW MORE?

Raminator

Raminator is a monster. It's 10 ft tall and 12.5 ft wide, and rides on 66-in-high tires weighing 900 lb each. It runs on the fuel methanol and guzzles it up very fast indeed. The average pickup does 20 to 30 miles on each gallon of fuel. On its high-speed runs, Raminator does just 250 *feet* per gallon—that is, it consumes 400 times as much fuel!

Shockwave

Les Shockley built the original Shockwave jet truck in 1984. It was his most challenging project, but he was already a famous drag racer, and his jet-powered dragsters had been setting records for years. His earlier Shockwave dragsters had been regularly hitting 350 mph, and in 1980, Shockley was the first ever to run the quarter-mile drag in less than 5 seconds.

The Dodge Ram

Ram has long been the name for Dodge's famously rugged pickups. Sculptor Avard T. Fairbanks hit upon the name in 1932, when he was asked to create a hood ornament for the latest Dodge pickup. He decided on a charging ram because, as he explained to Dodge engineers, "It is sure-footed; it's the King of the Trail; it won't be challenged by anything… And if you saw that ram charging down on you, what would you think? DODGE!"

Ford Raptor

The V8 Ford Raptor is a legend for its performance and speed off-road. But for 2017, Ford are introducing a new version with a V6 engine, boosted by twin turbochargers to 450 hp (compared to 411 for the V8). Ford claim that this "Ecoboost" engine will make the Raptor 25 percent faster. If so, the Raptor will be a superlative performer, roaring through the dirt.

NASCAR World Truck Series

One of the best places to see pickups racing bumper to bumper and wheel to wheel is in the NASCAR Camping World Truck Series. *NASCAR* stands for National Association for Stock Car Auto Racing, and the idea for the series dates back to 1991, when a group of off-road pickup-truck racers decided to compete on a paved track, as in Formula One racing.

Truck Racing

The first truck race was held on June 17, 1979, at the Atlanta Motor Speedway, and the idea quickly caught on, thanks to the 1977 movie *Smokey and the Bandit*. The movie stars Burt Reynolds as truck driver Bandit, who races his Kenworth truck from Texas to Georgia. There are now truck races all over the world, and most major truck manufacturers have their own racing teams.

INDEX

GLOSSARY

Bigfoot A competition truck with giant wheels, named after legendary creature of the woods Bigfoot

Brake horsepower (bhp) The power direct from the engine; 1 horsepower can move 550 pounds one foot every second, written as 550 ft-lb per second

Drag race A race against the clock in which vehicles cover a quarter of a mile from a standing start

Jet engine An engine that delivers a blast of hot gases to provide power rather than driving wheels around

Nitro A high-powered fuel based on nitromethane

Thrust The power of a jet engine

Torque The turning force of an engine, measured in pounds per feet (lb-ft)

V8 An engine with eight cylinders in two rows of four at a V-shaped angle

THE AUTHOR

John Farndon is Royal Literary Fellow at Anglia Ruskin University in Cambridge, UK. He has written a huge number of books for adults and children on science, technology, and nature, and has been shortlisted four times for the Royal Society's Young People's Book Prize.

THE ILLUSTRATORS

UK artist Mat Edwards has been drawing for as long as he can remember. He began his career with a four-year apprenticeship as a repro artist in the ceramic industry and has been a freelance illustrator since 1992.

Jeremy Pyke left the RAF to follow his passion for illustration. He has worked on many children's books and uses oil, watercolor, computer-generated illustration, and 3-D animation.

Picture Credits (abbreviations: t = top; b = bottom; c = center; l = left; r = right)

© www.shutterstock.com: 8 tc, 8 br, 9 cr, 9 bl

6 cl Natursports / Shutterstock.com.
7 tr Doug James / Shutterstock.com
9 tr i4lcocl2/www.Shutterstock.com.